MY FIRST BOOK
NEW ZEALAND

ALL ABOUT NEW ZEALAND FOR KIDS

GLOBED
CHILDREN BOOKS

Copyright 2023 by Penelope Palette

All rights reserved. No part of this book may be reproduced or distributed in any form without prior written permission from the author, with the exception of non-commercial uses permitted by copyright law.

Limited of Liability/Disclaimer of Warranty: The publisher and author make no representations or liabilities with respect to the accuracy and completeness of the contents of this work and specifically disclaim all warranties including without limitations warranties of fitness of particular purpose. No warranty may be created or extended by sales or promotional materials. This work is sold with the understanding that the publisher and author is not engaging in rendering medical, legal or any other professional advice or service. Further, readers should be aware that websites listed in this work may have changed or disappeared between when this work was written and when it is read.

Interior and cover Design: Daniel Day
Editor: Margaret Bam

For My Sons, Daniel, David and Jude

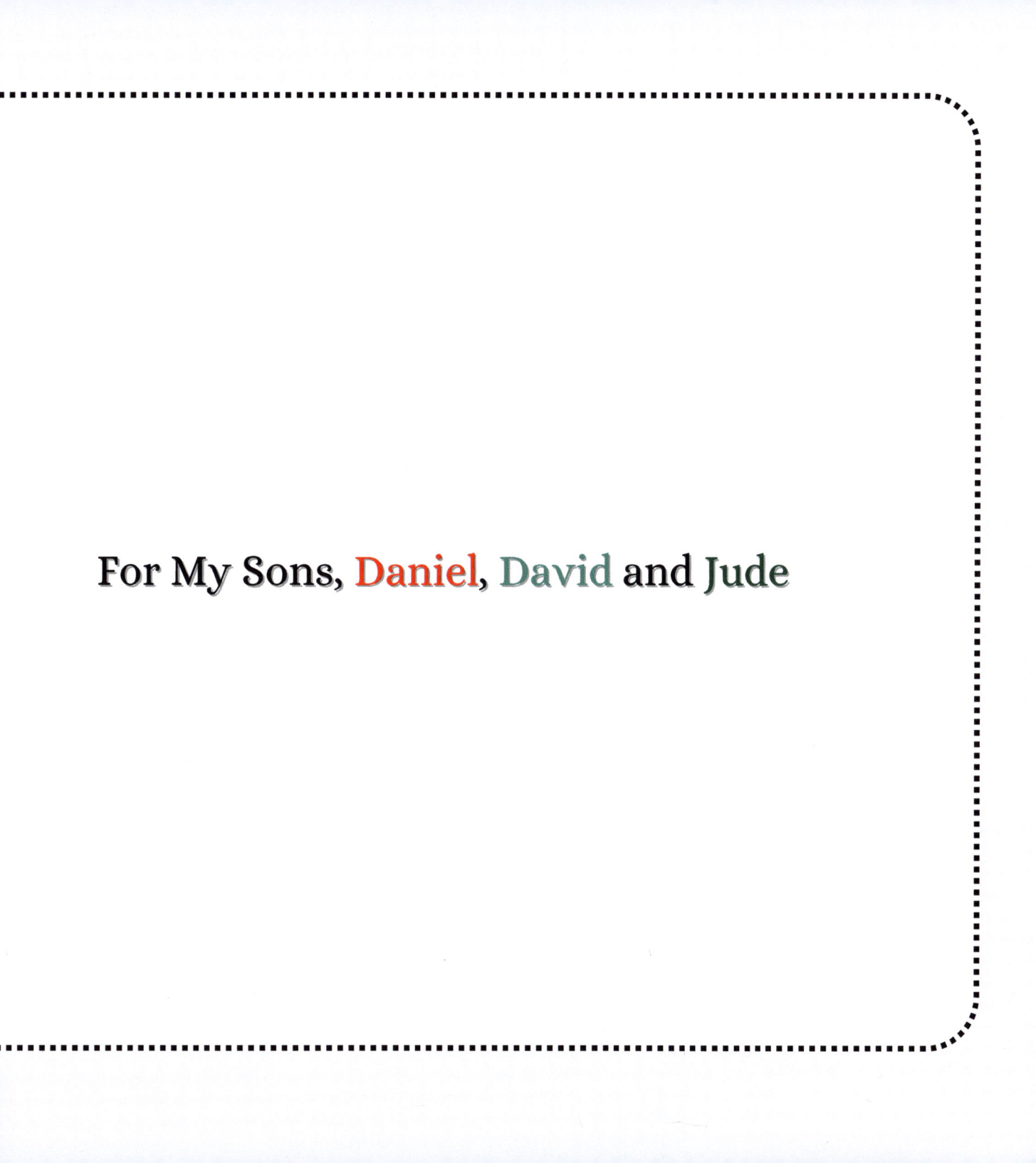

Auckland, New Zealand

New Zealand

New Zealand is an **island country.**

A country is land that is controlled by a **single government**. Countries are also called **nations, states, or nation-states**.

Countries can be **different sizes**. Some countries are big and others are small.

Auckland, New Zealand

Where Is New Zealand?

New Zealand is geographically located in the continent of **Oceania**.

A continent is **a massive area of land that is separated from others by water or other natural features**.

The country of New Zealand is situated in the southwestern Pacific Ocean and consists of two main landmasses—the North Island and the South Island and over 700 smaller islands.

Wellington, New Zealand

Capital

The capital of New Zealand is **Wellington.**

Wellington is located at the southern end of the North Island.

Auckland is also the largest city in New Zealand.

Queenstown, New Zealand

Regions

New Zealand is divided into 16 regions

The regions of New Zealand are

Northland, Auckland, Waikato, Bay of Plenty, Gisborne, Hawke's Bay, Taranaki, Manawatu-Whanganui, Wellington, Tasman, Nelson, Marlborough, West Coast, Canterbury, Otago, and Southland.

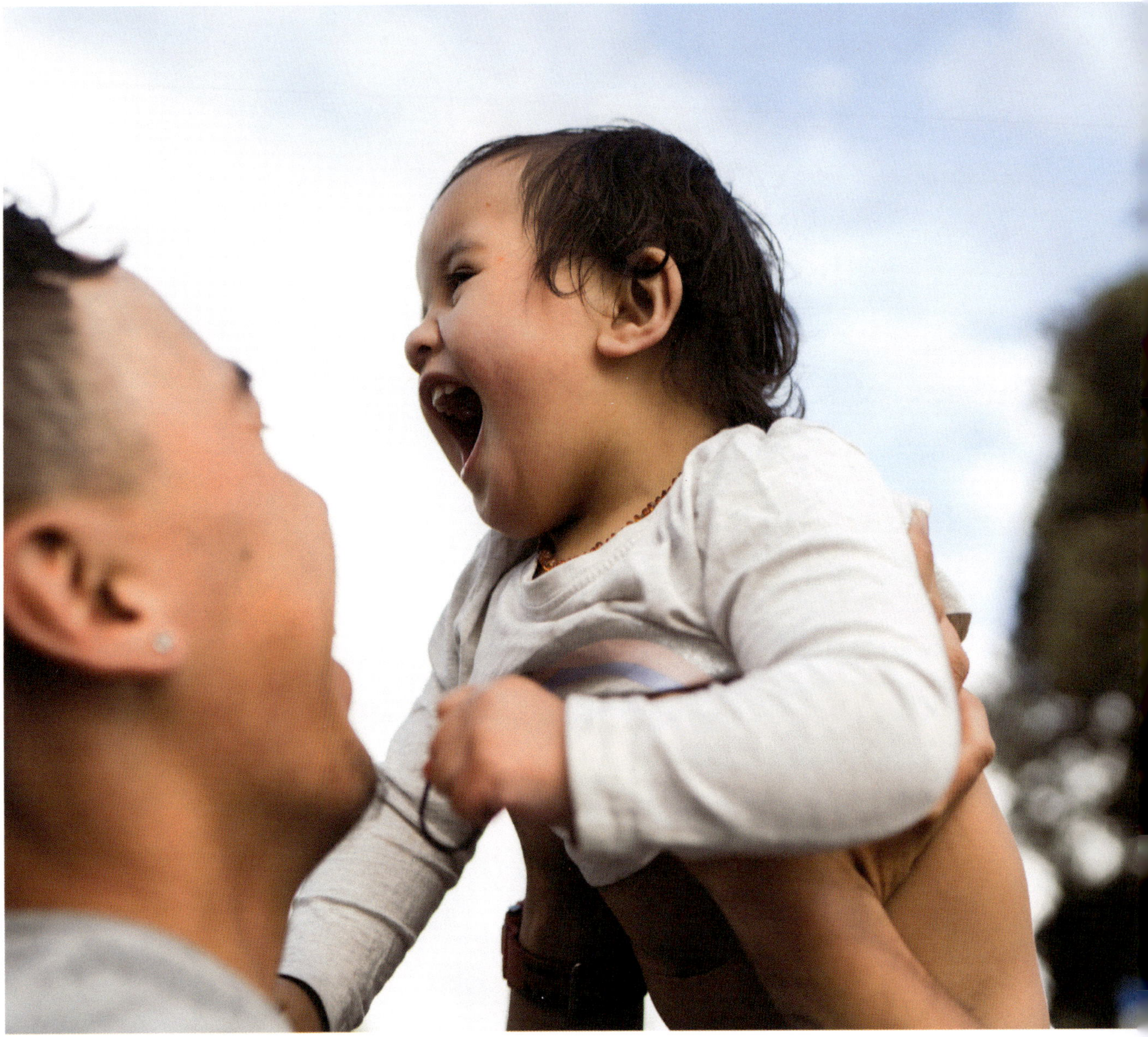

Population

New Zealand has population of around **5.1 million people.**

Auckland is the most populated city in New Zealand, with a population of over 1.6 million people. It is known for its stunning harbours, volcanic cones, and beautiful beaches.

Devonport, New Zealand

Size

New Zealand is **268,021 square kilometres** making it the 75th largest country in the world and the sixth-largest island country by area.

New Zealand is known for its stunning natural beauty, which includes mountains, beaches, forests, and fjords.

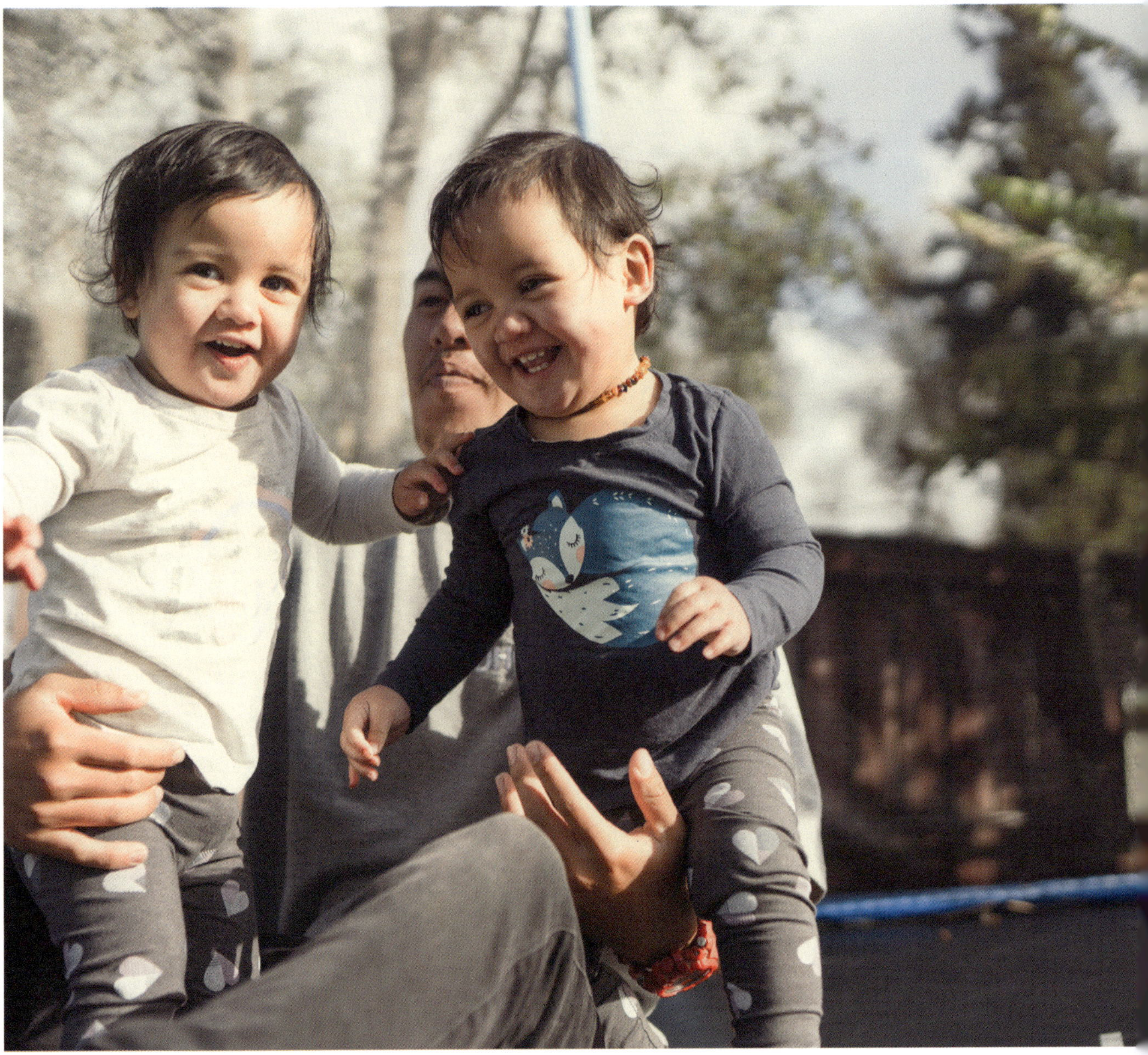

Languages

The official languages of New Zealand are English, Māori and NZ Sign Language. English is the most spoken language in the world with over a billion speakers.

Here are some Kiwi phrases
- **Kia Ora – Be well/healthy**
- **Sweet as – No problem/thank you/no worries**
- **Knackered – Really tired**
- **She'll be alright – "Whatever is wrong will right itself with time"**
- **Pack a sad – Throwing a tantrum**

Sky Tower, New Zealand

Attractions

There are lots of interesting places to see in New Zealand.

Some beautiful places to visit in New Zealand are

- Sky Tower
- Auckland War Memorial Museum
- Abel Tasman National Park
- Waiotapu Thermal Wonderland

Dunedin, New Zealand

History of New Zealand

New Zealand has a rich and long history. Before colonization, New Zealand was inhabited by the Maori people for over 1,000 years.

New Zealand was settled by the Polynesians in the 13th century. In 1840, the Treaty of Waitangi was signed between the British Crown and Maori chiefs, which established British sovereignty over New Zealand.

New Zealand gained independence from Britain in 1947, but King Charles III remains the head of state.

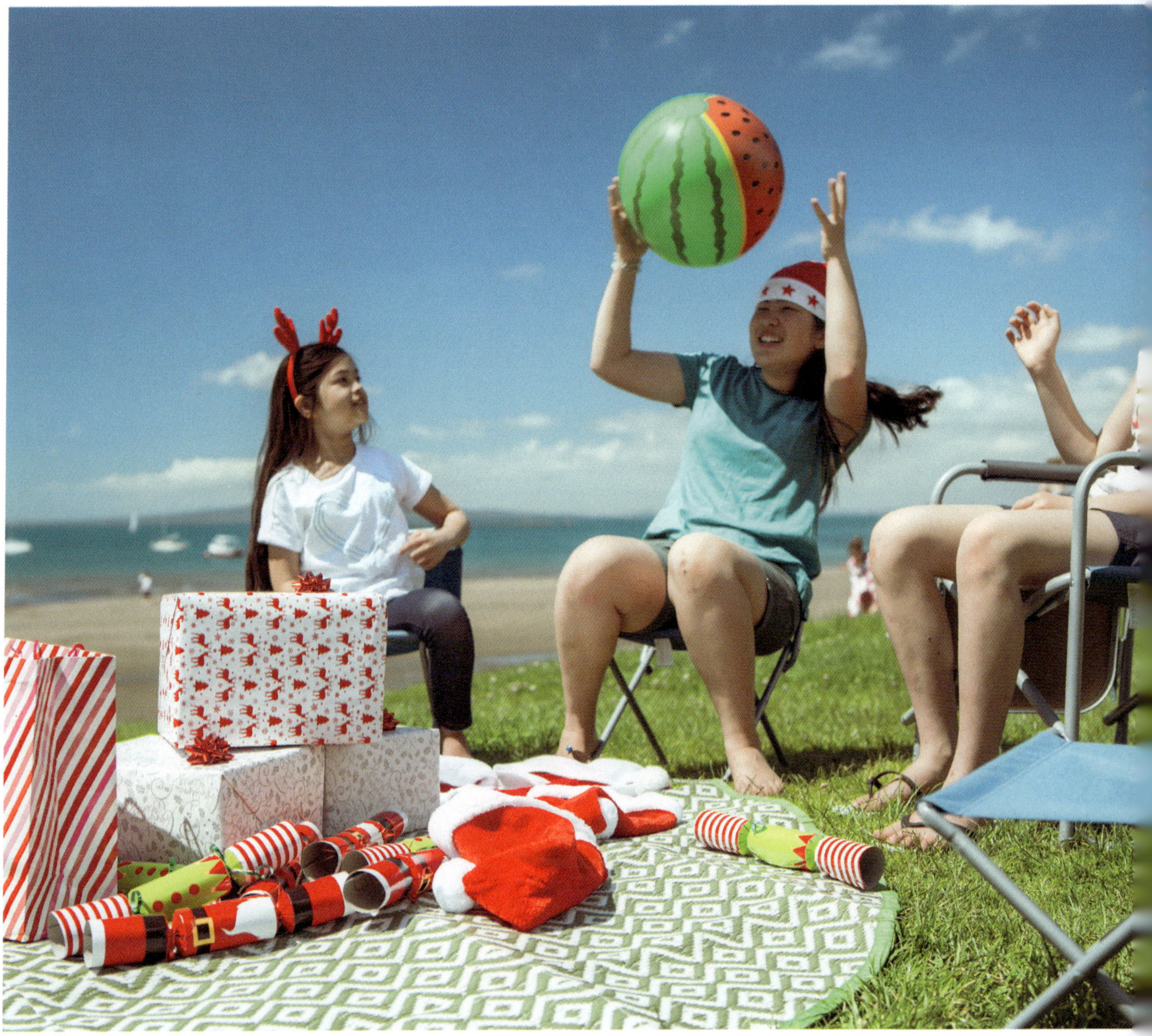

Customs in New Zealand

New Zealand has many fascinating customs and traditions.

- **Christmas is a widely celebrated holiday in New Zealand, and many people enjoy spending the day with family and friends, exchanging gifts, and enjoying a traditional Christmas dinner.**
- **Waitangi Day is a national holiday in New Zealand that is celebrated on February 6th each year. It commemorates the signing of the Treaty of Waitangi between the British Crown and Maori chiefs in 1840.**

Man playing in Queen Street, New Zealand

Music of New Zealand

New Zealand has a vibrant and diverse music scene, with many different genres and styles represented. Popular music genres in New Zealand such as **rock, pop, hip-hop, electronic music, and Maori music.** .

Some notable Kiwi musicians include
- **Lorde - A New Zealand singer and songwriter.**
- **Hayley Westenra - A New Zealand classical crossover singer and songwriter.**
- **Bic Runga - A New Zealand singer-songwriter and multi-instrumentalist pop artist.**

Meat pie

Food of New Zealand

New Zealand cuisine is diverse and influenced by the country's geography and cultural heritage

New Zealand does not have an official national dish, but some popular dishes include fish and chips, meat pies, pavlova, and hokey pokey ice cream.

Hangi

Food of New Zealand

New Zealand cuisine is a fusion of different cultures, including Maori, British, European, and Asian influences.

Popular dishes in New Zealand include

- **Fish and chips: A classic New Zealand dish consisting of battered and fried fish served with hot chips (fries).**
- **Meat pies: A savory pastry filled with minced meat, gravy, and sometimes vegetables.**
- **Hangi: A traditional Maori dish where meat and vegetables are cooked in an earth oven.**

South Island, New Zealand

Weather in New Zealand

Due to its location in the southern hemisphere, New Zealand experiences opposite seasons from the northern hemisphere. The country has a temperate climate, with mild temperatures and high rainfall.

The warmest month in New Zealand is typically January. During this time, the country experiences its summer season, with average temperatures ranging from 20-30 degrees Celsius in most parts of the country.

Kiwi bird

Animals of New Zealand

There are many wonderful animals in New Zealand.

Here are some animals that live in New Zealand

- **Kiwi**
- **Tuatara**
- **Kākāpō**
- **Kea**
- **Yellow-eyed penguin**
- **Sea lions**

Hot Water Beach, New Zealand

Beaches

There are many beautiful beaches in New Zealand which is one of the reasons why so many people visit this beautiful country every year.

Here are some beautiful beaches in New Zealand

- Hot Water Beach
- Piha Beach
- Ninety Mile Beach
- Gillespies Beach
- Koekohe Beach

Rugby player singing New Zealand National Anthem

Sports of New Zealand

Sports play an integral part in Kiwi culture. The most popular sports in New Zealand are **Football, Rugby, Soccer and Cricket.**

Here are some of famous sportspeople from New Zealand

- **Shane van Gisbergen - Formula one**
- **Scott Dixon - Formula one**
- **Jack Lovelock - Athletics**
- **Pero Cameron - Basketball**

Katherine Mansfield (1888 –1923)

Figures

There are many notable figures from New Zealand who have made significant contributions to their fields and to the world at large.

Here are some notable New Zealander figures

- **Sir Edmund Hillary: Mountaineer**
- **Russell Crowe - Actor**
- **Ernest Rutherford - Physicist**
- **Katherine Mansfield - Writer**

Rotorua Redwoods Forest, New Zealand

Something Extra...

As a little something extra, we are going to share some lesser known facts about New Zealand

- **New Zealand is home to the world's smallest dolphin, the Hector's dolphin.**
- **New Zealand has a long history of producing high-quality wines, particularly Sauvignon Blanc and Pinot Noir.**
- **The national bird of New Zealand is the kiwi, a flightless bird that is found only in the country.**

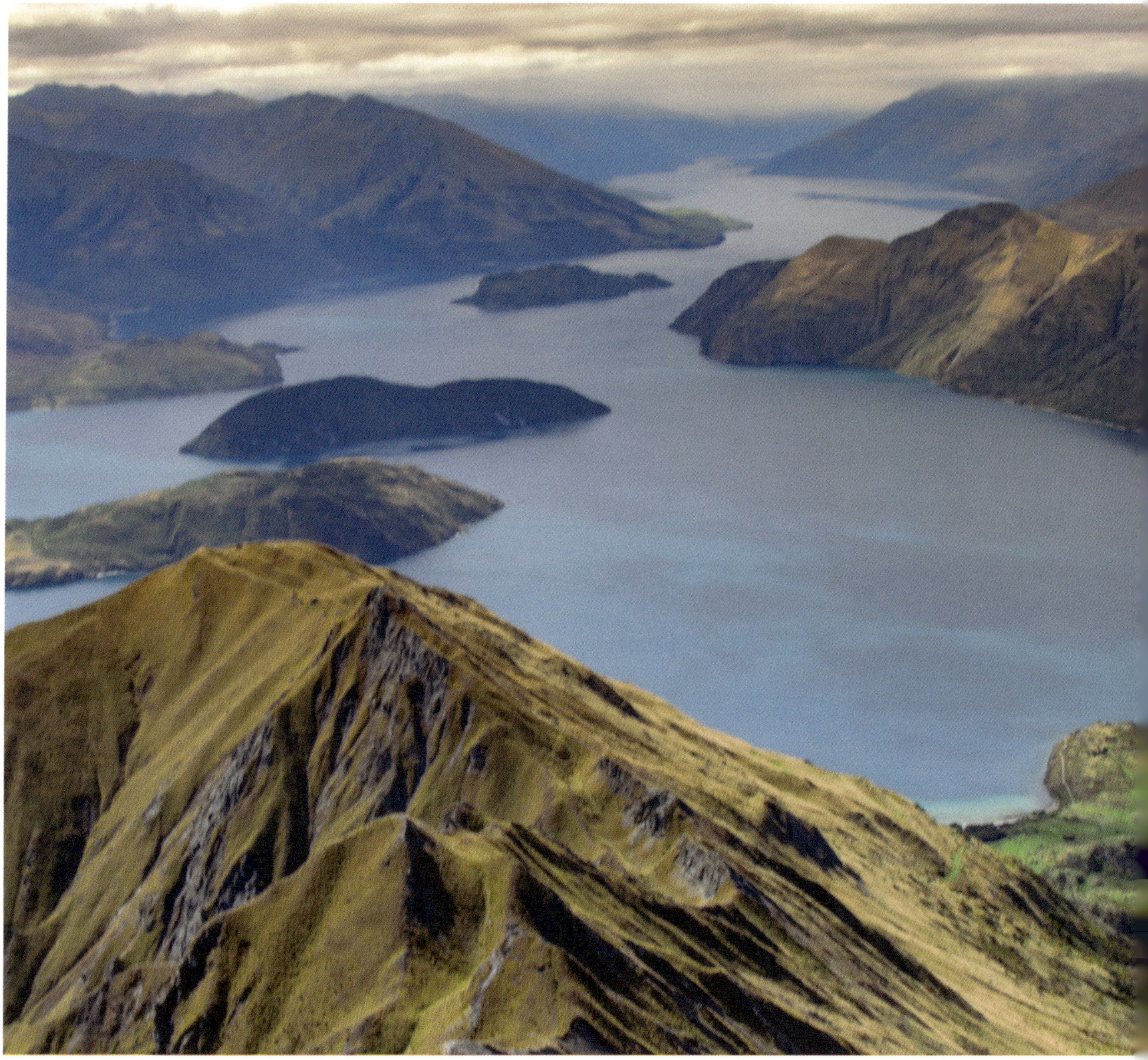

Words From the Author

We hope that you enjoyed learning about the wonderful island of New Zealand.

New Zealand is a country rich in culture and beauty, with lots of wonderful places to visit and people to meet.

We hope you continue to learn more about this wonderful nation. If you enjoyed this book, consider leaving a review!

With Love

Printed in Great Britain
by Amazon